Weapons of War

Tracey Turner

EDGE FRANKLIN WATTS

LONDON·SYDNEY

First published in 2013 by
Franklin Watts
338 Euston Road
London NW1 3BH

Franklin Watts Australia
Level 17/207 Kent Street
Sydney NSW 2000

Text © Tracey Turner 2013
Design © Franklin Watts 2013

Series editor: Adrian Cole
Art direction: Peter Scoulding
Design: D R Ink
Picture research: Diana Morris

Warning! This is not a normal book!

Acknowledgements:
Alexander Babich/Shutterstock: front cover b, back cover t.
Biblioteca Nacional de Madrid: 6. John Braid/Shutterstock: 8.
Martin Brayley/Dreamstime: 11, 23. Jose Gil/Shutterstock: 18r.
Rafael Laguillo/Dreamstime: 13. Edward Parker/Alamy: 17.
Paulo M.F. Pires/Shutterstock: front cover t. Nikolay Pozdeev/
Dreamstime: 20. U.S. Air Force Photo/Jeff Fisher: 10.
U.S Air Force Photo/Master Sgt. Lorenzo Gaines : 5. U.S Air Force Photo/
Master Sgt. Kevin Grunewald: 7. U.S Air Force Photo/Staff Sgt. Christopher
Hubenthal: title, 19. U.S. Air Force Photo/ Lt.Col. Leslie Pratt: 14.
U.S. Army Photo: 9. U.S.Army Photo/Tech.Sgt. Andy Dunaway: 12.
U.S. Marine Corps/Cpl. Jeff Drew: 15. U.S. Navy Photo/
Lt. j.g. Monika Hess: 16.bU.S. Navy Photo/Photographers Mate 3rd Class
Ramon Preciad Presdiado: 21. wacpan/Shutterstock: 18. Robert Wisdom/
Dreamstime: 22. Zim235/Dreamstime: 4.

Every attempt has been made to clear copyright. Should there be any
inadvertent omission please apply to the publisher for rectification.

A CIP catalogue record for this book
is available from the British Library.

Dewey Classification: 355.8

ISBN: 978 1 4451 1447 7

Printed in China

Franklin Watts is a division of Hachette
Children's Books, an Hachette UK company.
www.hachette.co.uk

Contents

Please note: every effort has been made by the Publishers to ensure
that the websites in this book contain no inappropriate or offensive
material. However, because of the nature of the Internet, it is impossible to
guarantee that the contents of these sites will not be altered. We strongly
advise that Internet access is supervised by a responsible adult.

Ultimate 20 is not just a book where you can find out loads of facts and stats about fantastic stuff – it's also a brilliant game book!

How to play

1.
Grab a copy of *Ultimate 20* – oh, you have. OK, now get your friends to grab a copy, too.

2.
Each player closes their eyes and flicks to a game page. Now, open your eyes and choose one of the Ultimate 20. Decide who goes first, then that person reads out what weapon they've chosen, plus the name of the stat. For example, this player has chosen the Attack Helicopter and the Power stat, with an Ultimate 20 ranking of 6.

> **AH-64 Apache Attack Helicopter**
> **Weight:** 5,165 kg   *14*
> **Maximum range:** ~~3,701 km~~   *6*
> **Power:** High   *6*
> **Accuracy:** Very good   *5*
> **Cost:** £17,850,000   *17*

3.
Now, challenge your friends to see who has the highest-ranking stat – the lower the number (from 1–20) the better your chances of winning. (1 = good, 20 = goofy).

Player 1

Power: High	6

Player 2

Power: Low	17

4.
Whoever has the lowest number is the winner – nice one! If you have the same number – you've tied.

Time to flick, choose, challenge again!

(If you land on the same game page, choose the Ultimate 20 listing opposite.)

Mash it up!

If you haven't got the same *Ultimate 20* book as your friends, you can **STILL** play — Ultimate 20 Mash Up! The rules are the same as the regular game (above), so flick and choose one of your Ultimate 20 and a stat, then read them out. Each player does this. Now read out the Ultimate 20 ranking to see whose choice is the best. Can Julius Caesar beat a werewolf? Can Bobby Charlton beat a king cobra snake?

Assault Rifle

Assault rifles are hand-held guns that can fire single shots or automatic bursts of bullets. Most troops around the world today use some sort of assault rifle.

Early development

Assault rifles began to be developed from machine guns at the beginning of the 20th century. The first assault rifle was used by the German army at the end of World War II (1939–45).

Kalashnikov – AK-47

The AK-47 is the most famous, and most widely used, assault rifle. It was developed by the USSR (modern-day Russia) and used by the Soviet army in 1949. The AK-47 is fairly cheap to make, reliable and easy to maintain. It packs a deadly punch, too — firing 600 rounds per minute — although it's not as accurate as some assault rifles.

Rifle technology

The very latest assault rifles have a range of up to 600 metres. They are equipped with night vision and telescopic sights, and some have a grenade launcher underneath the rifle barrel.

AK-47 Assault Rifle

6

Weight: 4.78 kg (loaded)

14

Maximum Range: 350 m

12

Power: Medium

16

Accuracy: Average

7

Cost: £350 (average)

Intercontinental Ballistic Missile

Intercontinental ballistic missiles, or ICBMs, are missiles with a range of more than 5,600 kilometres. That's roughly the distance between London and New York. Scarily, these continent-crossing missiles are designed to carry nuclear warheads.

Rocket technology

ICBMs were developed from rocket technology. The first successful rocket-powered missile was the German-designed V-2, which had a range of just 350 km. In 1957, the USSR successfully flew its R-7 missile more than 6,000 km. It was the world's first ICBM. The Soviets used a similar rocket to put the first human into space!

LGM-30 Minuteman III

Weight: 35,300 kg   **18**

Maximum Range: 13,000 km (est.)   **3**

Power: Very high   **2**

Accuracy: Very good   **1**

Cost: £7,000,000   **16**

Multiple strikes

Modern long-range ballistic missiles (like the Minuteman on the right) carry several nuclear warheads. These can accurately strike several targets at once. They can either be launched from land – from silos or from heavy lorries – or from submarines. Either way, we hope no one ever uses these weapons of mass destruction!

Greek Fire

Fire has been used as a weapon for thousands of years: flaming arrows, hand-thrown fire pots, and flaming missiles fired from catapults. But when Greek fire was invented in the 7th century CE, no one had seen anything like it.

Top-secret recipe

Greek fire was invented in Constantinople (modern-day Istanbul), part of the Byzantine Empire. The inventor was a Syrian engineer called Callinicus. The secret of how to make Greek fire was kept for hundreds of years, but the recipe vanished with the Byzantine Empire. Today people think it contained sulphur, charcoal, liquid petroleum and quicklime.

Terrifying fire power

Greek fire could be put into pots and thrown by hand, or shot at the enemy through tubes, like a flamethrower. It was said to be impossible to put out, and even burned on water. It terrified many of the Byzantine Empire's enemies over the centuries.

Greek Fire

Weight: 240 kg (excluding a 875 kg cauldron) **10**
Maximum Range: 15 m **18**
Power: Low **18**
Accuracy: Poor **19**
Cost: Expensive at the time **6**

Bomber Aircraft

Different kinds of aircraft are used in warfare: fighters, bombers, spy planes and attack aircraft. Bombers are huge aircraft designed to carry large payloads – usually bombs – to destroy targets such as harbours or even cities.

Bomber power

The first bombers appeared in World War I (1914–1918). By World War II they had become huge, powerful and capable of dropping devastating bombs. Large cities were targeted, causing widespread damage and loss of life.

B-52 bomber

B-52s are probably the most famous bomber aircraft of all time. Modern B-52s are nearly 50 m long, and are powered by jet engines. They can carry a payload of up to 32,000 kg. They're expected to continue flying for the US Airforce into the 2040s.

B-52 Stratofortress

Weight: 83,250 kg	20
Maximum Range: 14,162 km	2
	5
Power: High	9
Accuracy: Good	
Cost: £32,855,471	18

Chlorine Gas

Chlorine gas was first used in warfare during World War I. It is a chemical that causes a slow, painful death. It's considered to be one of the most terrible weapons of war ever.

Chlorine Gas **1**

Weight: 0.07 kg (molecular weight) **20**

Maximum Range: Variable **11**

Power: High **20**

Accuracy: Poor **8**

Cost: ??

Gas attack

The gas was used for the first time in 1915, when Allied soldiers saw a strange-smelling, greenish-yellow mist approaching from the German side. Many of them quickly became unable to breathe, and suffocated to death. During World War I both sides used chlorine gas – as well as mustard gas, and the even more deadly phosgene gas. At first, urine-soaked pads were used to defend soldiers from the gas – not a great solution! Before long, though, troops were given gas masks (right), which were much more effective against chemicals.

Banned gas

In 1925, a treaty called the Geneva Protocol banned the use of deadly gas (chemical weapons), as well as weapons that spread harmful bacteria (biological weapons). Despite the ban, chemical weapons have still been used in wars.

Tank

Tanks are heavily armoured vehicles armed with an enormous gun at the front. Their tracks help them cross ground that few other vehicles could cover, and the soldiers inside are well protected from attack.

World War I tanks

Tanks were invented in Britain and first used in warfare in 1916, during World War I. These "Mark One" tanks took inspiration from an early design called Little Willie. They were armed with 57-mm naval guns and machine guns, and could travel at a maximum speed of just six km/h.

Modern tanks – M1A1 Abrams

Modern tanks are much faster, more powerful and more reliable. In 1985, the first M1A1 Abrams tank was produced in the USA. It features a 120-mm gun and can travel at up to 72 km/h. It is protected against chemical, biological and nuclear attack. Some versions of the M1A1 Abrams are fitted with spectral camouflage, making it harder for them to be detected.

M1A1 Abrams Tank

Weight: 61,325 kg	19
Maximum Range: 426 km	9
Power: High	6
Accuracy: Good	9
Cost: £5,279,025	15

Nuclear Weapons

Nuclear weapons are the most powerful weapons on Earth. Their destructive energy comes from nuclear reactions, producing a massive shockwave, extreme heat and deadly radiation.

"Little Boy" Nuclear Bomb

Weight: 4,400 kg — *13*

Maximum Range: 1.6 km (blast range) — *1*

Power: Very high — *1*

Accuracy: Very good — *1*

Cost: £185,000,000 — *20*

Devastating effects

Nuclear weapons have the power to cause widespread, long-term destruction. After a nuclear explosion, the ground is contaminated with radiation, and people who survive the initial blast become sick with radiation poisoning.

Hiroshima and Nagasaki

Only two nuclear bombs have been dropped in warfare. In 1945, to end World War II, the USA dropped "Little Boy" on Hiroshima and another nuclear bomb called "Fat Man" on Nagasaki, Japan. Over 200,000 people died and the towns were completely destroyed.

Nuclear powers

Since 1945, around nine countries have developed even more powerful nuclear bombs. These are China, France, India, Israel, North Korea, Pakistan, Russia, the UK and the USA.

Machine Gun

Machine guns are super-powerful guns, capable of firing more than fifteen bullets a second. They're designed to keep firing bullets for as long as the trigger is held down (until the ammunition runs out).

Maxim Gun ("Sokolov" M1910 variant) **7**

Weight: 23.8 kg (excluding shield and wheels) **11**

Maximum Range: 2.7 km **12**

Power: Medium **15**

Accuracy: Good **9**

Cost: £4,000 (est.)

Maxim gun

The Maxim gun was the first machine gun, invented by Sir Hiram Stephens Maxim in 1884. Even then it could fire 600 bullets a minute. Maxims were heavy and took a team of soldiers to operate. They were widely used until the end of World War I.

Using recoil energy

When a gun is fired, an explosion inside the gun makes the bullet shoot out of the barrel. The force of the explosion also makes the gun move backwards, called "recoil". Maxim guns used the recoil energy to eject the spent bullet cartridge and insert the next bullet.

Modern machine guns

Today there are different types of machine gun. Some light machine guns can be hand-held. Other, heavier ones, need a tripod or are mounted on a vehicle, such as a tank.

Attack Helicopter

Helicopters were invented in 1936, and first appeared in warfare during World War II. Since then they've become essential for transporting troops and supplies, and as attack aircraft.

Aerial advantages

Helicopters have some advantages over fixed-wing planes: they can land and take off vertically, so they don't need runways. This allows them to operate in remote areas and cities. However, helicopters are generally slower than other attack aircraft, so they're more vulnerable to attack.

Attack helicopter – Apache

The Apache is the United States' main attack helicopter, and has been in service since the 1980s. The aircraft has two huge Rolls Royce engines, each with 2,100 horsepower. It is armed with a M230 30-mm cannon, and can launch a range of rockets and missiles. Other features include night vision, radar and target tracking.

AH-64 Apache Attack Helicopter

Weight: 5,165 kg	14
Maximum Range: 1,800 km	6
Power: High	6
Accuracy: Very good	5
Cost: £17,850,000	17

Trebuchet

A trebuchet is a missile-flinging machine used during the Middle Ages. Counterweight trebuchets were used to attack besieged castles – mainly to smash holes in the stone walls.

Bashing buildings

Trebuchets used a long arm with a container for the missile at one end, and a heavy load at the other. The load would pull down the arm, flinging the missile (usually a heavy piece of stone) into the air. Once a trebuchet was built, it couldn't be moved very easily, so they were only really used during a siege.

Counterweight Trebuchet

Weight: 22,000 kg (including counterweight)	17
Range: 300 m (est.)	16
Power: Low	17
Accuracy: Average	16
Cost: £300	3

Gruesome missiles

Missiles didn't just include stones: barrels of tar could be set on fire and hurled at the target, and burning sand was sometimes thrown. More gruesome missiles were thrown too, such as dung, dead animals and dead people. Yuck! These helped to spread disease in the town under attack.

Unmanned Aerial Vehicles

These aircraft, also called UAVs or drones, don't have a pilot on board. Instead they're either flown by a pilot on the ground, by remote control, or they can fly by themselves according to a programmed flight plan. UAVs are used in warfare for spying and for attack, without risking the lives of a human crew.

Deadly Predator

The Predator is one of the most famous types of UAV. The aircraft is equipped with satellite navigation, radar, and video equipment including an infrared camera for night-time vision. It can carry over 200 kg of weapons, which might be air-to-ground or air-to-air missiles, and can keep flying for up to 40 hours.

UAV remote pilot

A Predator pilot flies the plane using controls that transmit via satellite links. He or she relies on the cameras aboard the plane to see what's going on. Visability is limited, but targeting equipment means that weapons can be used accurately.

MQ-1 Predator UAV

Weight: 512 kg	11
Maximum Range: 1,200 km	7
Power: High	8
Accuracy: Very good	5
Cost: £2,700,000	14

Cannon

Cannons are big guns that use explosive energy to launch a projectile – you know – a cannonball! They changed warfare across the world.

Chinese origins

Cannon technology spread from China in the 12th century, into the Middle East and Europe. There they replaced wooden siege weapons, such as the trebuchet (see page 13). In the 1300s, bombard cannons were about 1.5 m long. They could fire cannonballs weighing 45 kg.
By the 1500s, some cannons had barrels three metres long, and weighed around eight tonnes – more than an African elephant.

M198 Howitzer	
Weight: 7,154 kg	**15**
Maximum Range: 22.4 km	**9**
Power: High	**8**
Accuracy: Average	**11**
Cost: £324,455	**11**

Modern cannon – M198 howitzer

The modern equivalent of medieval cannon are big artillery weapons such as the M198 howitzer. It has a range of up to 22.5 km and a firing rate of about four per minute, depending on the missile – much faster than the cannon of the Middle Ages!

Cruise Missile

Cruise missiles are flying bombs that can make their own way to a target. They can strike an enemy many kilometres away, using the missile's onboard navigation system.

Missile development

During World War II Germany developed the first cruise missiles: V-1s, also known as "buzz bombs". V-1s bombed cities without any pilots risking their lives. The United States and the Soviet Union both developed cruise missiles in the 1960s and 70s: they could carry either conventional or nuclear warheads.

Tomahawk cruise missile

Tomahawk cruise missiles were first developed in the 1970s and are still in use today. They were designed to be launched from sea or land, though today they are all sea-launched. They can speed through the air at around 880 km/h, with a range of up to 2,500 km.

Tomahawk Cruise Missile

Weight: 1,300 kg — 12

Maximum Range: 2,500 km — 5

Power: Very high — 3

Accuracy: Very good — 1

Cost: £890,000 — 13

Longbow

Bows and arrows are some of the first weapons ever invented. In the Middle Ages a new type of bow – the longbow – became the most important weapon of the Hundred Years' War (1337–1453).

Longbow (English)

2

Weight: 0.60 kg

13

Maximum Range: 410 m

19

Power: Low

12

Accuracy: Good

3

Cost: £300

Accurate archers

Medieval longbows were about 1.8 m long and used metre-long arrows. Longbow archers needed a lot of strength to draw the bow. Longbows had a range of 300 m or more, and skilled longbow archers could accurately shoot up to 12 arrows a minute.

Hundred Years' War

The longbow played a key part in deciding battles between England and France during this period (even though it wasn't actually 100 years). At the Battle of Crécy in 1346, the English were outnumbered but still won the battle. The English longbow archers were more effective than the French crossbowmen.

Samurai Sword

A Samurai sword – or *katana* – was the main weapon of Japanese Samurai. Samurai were originally bodyguards for Japanese lords, and later became a highly respected warrior class. Samurai were at their height in the 1400s and 1500s, the Era of Warring States in Japan.

Samurai Sword

Weight: 1 kg

Maximum Range: 1 m — 4

Power: Medium — 19

Accuracy: Very good — 15

Cost: £4,000 (average) — 4

9

Slicing swords

The Samurai sword was the most famous Samurai weapon. It was long and curved (up to about 70 cm long), with a single-edged blade. Each sword had a large hilt, often beautifully decorated, which was designed to be held with two hands. The sword was worn in the Samurai's belt, blade side up, and an accomplished Samurai warrior could draw his sword and strike an opponent in one fluid motion.

Scary Samurai

Samurai in their full armour looked terrifying. They had an array of other weapons, including a metal chain with handles at either end, called a *manriki-gusari*; a huge metal truncheon, called a *jutte*; or an iron fan, called a *tessen*. From the 1500s onwards, Samurai also had guns.

Stealth Fighter Aircraft

Modern fighter planes fly faster than the speed of sound and are armed with deadly missiles, guns and bombs. They use stealth technology to hide from the enemy.

The first fighters

The first war planes flew during World War I. The pilots of early fighter planes fired at one another with pistols, or even threw bricks! Modern fighter planes are much faster and better equipped. The F-22 Raptor is capable of nearly twice the speed of sound, that's a whopping 2,450 km/h! It's armed with a 20-mm cannon and a combination of missiles and bombs.

Hidden menace

Modern fighter planes are difficult to detect by the enemy. The shape of the planes, and the radio-wave absorbing material they use, keeps them hidden from radar. They're also specially cooled to reduce the threat of heat-seeking missiles.

F-22 Raptor	
Weight: 19,700 kg	16
Maximum Range: 2,960 km	4
Power: Very high	4
Accuracy: Very good	5
Cost: £92,000,000	19

Crossbow

The crossbow is a mechanised version of the bow and arrow. During the Middle Ages, it was one of the most successful missile weapons.

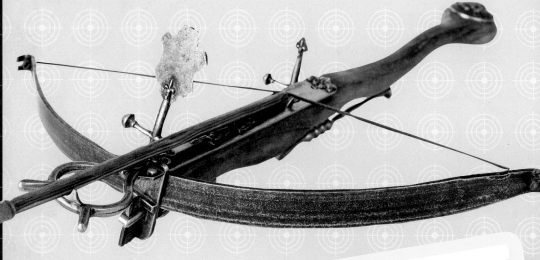

Crossbow (pull lever)	5
Weight: 2.5 kg	14
Maximum Range: 350 m	19
Power: Low	12
Accuracy: Good	2
Cost: £250	

Deadly bolts

The crossbow is a super-powerful metal bow. Bolts, or quarrels, are loaded and can be released at speeds of 350 km/h. A bolt could easily pierce through chain mail at a distance of 300 m. There were different types of crossbow, some heavier and more powerful than others, but they were all easy to use and carry around, and highly accurate.

Medieval crossbows

Crossbows were invented in or near China around 500 BCE. The ancient Greeks and Romans both used crossbows. In Europe during the Middle Ages crossbows were especially widely used – they had advantages over the longbow, because it was much easier to train someone to use them. Eventually, guns took over from crossbows.

Torpedo

Torpedoes are self-propelled weapons that operate underwater, exploding when they strike or are close to their target. The name "torpedo" comes from a type of fish.

Early torpedoes

Torpedoes were developed in the late 1800s. Early ones could only travel about 650 m, and at a snail's pace of 11 km/h. A Turkish ship became the first to be sunk by a torpedo in 1878, during the Russo-Turkish War (1877–78). By 1914, the largest torpedoes contained 320 kilograms of explosives. Modern torpedoes have a range of around 10 km and travel at speeds of around 70 km/h.

Submarine torpedoes

Ships and aircraft have both been used to launch torpedoes, but torpedoes fired by submarines have been the most effective. During World War II, huge numbers of ships were sunk by torpedoes, many of them launched by German U-boats.

USN MK-46 Mod 5 Torpedo

Weight: 231 kg — 9

Maximum Range: 11 km — 10

Power: High — 10

Accuracy: Very good — 8

Cost: £600,000 — 12

War Chariot

War chariots are carriages on two spoked wheels, pulled by a team of two or more horses. They were the most powerful weapon of the Bronze Age (c.3300 BCE – c.1200 BCE).

Chariot team

Chariots were usually manned by a driver, who controlled the horses, and an archer, who shot arrows from a short bow. They were used across Central Asia, Europe, the Middle East, Egypt, India and the Far East. Scythed chariots, with sharp, sword-like scythes sticking out of the wheel axles, were used by the Persians.

War Chariot (Egyptian)

Weight: 35 kg — 8

Maximum Range: 12 km — 12

Power: Low — 16

Accuracy: Average — 16

Cost: Expensive at the time — 3

Massive battle

The Battle of Qadesh, between the Egyptians and the Hittites in 1274 BCE, was probably the biggest chariot battle ever. Up to six thousand chariots took part in the battle. Egyptian chariots were lightweight, and carried two men, making them fast. Heavier Hittite chariots were armoured and carried three men: a driver, archer and shieldbearer.

Hand Grenade

A hand grenade is a small bomb that can be thrown by hand. Early versions used during World War I contained gas, but most modern grenades are packed with deadly explosive.

Gunpowder grenades

The first explosive hand grenades were made in the 10th century in China, where gunpowder was invented. These were ceramic or metal containers filled with gunpowder. A fuse had to be lit before the grenade was thrown, so the person throwing the grenade wasn't always safe.

Mills Bomb

Weight: 0.76 kg — *3*

Maximum Range: 90 m (blast range) — *17*

Power: Medium — *14*

Accuracy: Average — *15*

Cost: £20 — *1*

Mills Bomb

Invented in 1915, the Mills Bomb was the first "safe" fragmentation hand grenade. Once the ring and pin (see above right) was pulled, there was a delay of about six seconds before the grenade exploded. Grenades could be thrown up to 30 metres, but the metal fragments of the exploding grenade could be blown 90 metres away!

Glossary

Allied – the name for the group of countries, including Britain and France, who fought Germany and other countries during the world wars

Byzantine Empire – the empire that ruled lands in the eastern Mediterranean region for a thousand years, from around 330 to 1453

chlorine gas – a chemical weapon that burns the lining of the lungs

payload – the total quantity of bombs or other goods carried by an aeroplane or flying missile

radar – using radio waves to detect the location of an object and the speed that it is travelling

radiation poisoning – life-threatening illness caused by exposure to the radiation released by a nuclear bomb

range – the distance that a weapon can fire its missiles

rounds per minute – how fast a weapon can fire or launch its bullets or missiles

silo – an underground container for a nuclear weapon

spectral camouflage – painting or printing patterns designed to prevent detection by radar or thermal-imaging cameras

stealth technology – materials specially designed to avoid detection by radar or any other electronic system

telescopic sights – a small telescope on a gun, used to pin-point a target accurately

treaty – an agreement drawn up between countries

weapons of mass destruction – a chemical, biological or radioactive weapon.

Index